YOU CHOOSE™
BOOKS

THE STORY OF

JUNETEENTH

An Interactive History Adventure

by Steven Otfinoski

Consultant:
Kenneth Goings
Professor of African-American and African Studies
The Ohio State University

CAPSTONE PRESS
a capstone imprint

You Choose Books are published by Capstone Press,
1710 Roe Crest Drive, North Mankato, Minnesota 56003
www.capstonepub.com

**Library of Congress Cataloging-in-Publication Data**
Otfinoski, Steven.
The story of Juneteenth: an interactive history adventure / by Steven Otfinoski
pages cm.
Summary: "In You Choose format, explores the history of Juneteenth Day, including
the Emancipation Proclamation, the post-Civil War South, and efforts to end
racism"—Provided by publisher.
Includes bibliographical references and index.
ISBN 978-1-4914-1802-4 (library binding)
ISBN 978-1-4914-1804-8 (paperback)
ISBN 978-1-4914-1806-2 (eBook PDF)
1. Juneteenth—Juvenile literature. 2. African Americans—Texas—Galveston—Social
life and customs—Juvenile literature. 3. Slaves—Emancipation—United States—
Juvenile literature. 4. African Americans—Anniversaries, etc.—Juvenile literature.
5. African Americans—Social life and customs—Juvenile literature. 6. Galveston
(Tex.)—Social life and customs—Juvenile literature. I. Title.
E185.93.T4O85 2015
305.896'073—dc23                                        2014024620

**Editorial Credits**

Kristen Mohn, editor; Bobbie Nuytten, designer; Wanda Winch, media researcher;
Charmaine Whitman, production specialist

**Photo Credits**

Art Resource, N.Y.: Michael Escoffery, cover; Austin History Center, Austin Public
Library, ID PICA 05481,102; Bridgeman Images: Peter Newark American Pictures/
Private Collection, 53; Capstone, 6; Getty Images: George Eastman House, 38,
Hulton Archive, 88, MPI, 92; Library of Congress: Prints and Photographs Division,
8, 15, 20, 40, 42, 47, 70, 81; North Wind Picture Archives, 12, 24, 32, 59, 67, 77,
100; Shutterstock: Oleg Iatsun, labels design, Roman Sigaev, parchment paper,
Sergiy Telesh, parchment roll design

Printed in Canada.
092014    008478FRS15

# TABLE OF CONTENTS

# About Your Adventure

YOU live in a nation divided by war. The end of the Civil War, in 1865, brings an end to slavery in the United States. The defeated southern states are ordered to release all slaves. How will they handle their freedom? What choices would you make?

In this book you'll explore how the choices people made meant the difference between life and death. The events you'll experience happened to real people.

Chapter One sets the scene. Then you choose which path to read. Follow the directions at the bottom of each page. The choices you make will change your outcome. After you finish one path, go back and read the others for new perspectives and more adventures.

*YOU CHOOSE the path*
*you take through history.*

On June 19, 1865, Texas slaves learned of their freedom. In the following years, many began to make their way north, looking for new lives.

# Jubilation

Free at last! April 9, 1865, was a historic day in American history. Confederate general Robert E. Lee surrendered to Union general Ulysses S. Grant at a farmhouse in the small Virginia settlement of Appomattox Court House. The long Civil War that divided America was coming to an end. Slavery, one major cause of the war, was abolished in the United States.

Southern plantation owners had to free their slaves by order of the federal government. However, slavery did not end everywhere. Texas, the most western of the Confederate states, was removed from much of the fighting. Many slave owners in Texas refused to release their slaves.

Gordon Granger read "General Order No. 3," mandating freedom to slaves and an "absolute equality ... between former masters and slaves."

The federal government sent General Gordon Granger to Texas with 2,000 troops to enforce emancipation. Granger arrived in the city of Galveston on June 18, 1865, placing the city and the state under military occupation.

The next day, June 19, Granger read "General Order No. 3," calling for the freeing of all slaves. Slave owners had no choice but to comply with the law.

Freed at last, former slaves danced in the streets of Galveston. For them June 19 became as important as the day the war ended. It came to be called "Juneteenth."

The newly freed people responded in different ways to their newfound freedom. Some followed the order's recommendation to stay on the plantations as hired workers for the same masters they served as slaves.

Others left their plantations looking for jobs in the area. Still others headed to larger towns and cities, which they hoped would offer them better opportunities. Some young blacks, including children, agreed to work as apprentices on plantations run by former slave owners.

*Turn the page.*

Though slavery was abolished, prejudice and racism against blacks continued. Many southern whites resented the newly freed people. They were afraid the former slaves would take their jobs. Whites created laws called "Black Codes" to restrict their progress. Racist groups like the Ku Klux Klan, formed in 1866, terrorized and murdered many black people.

Not all white southerners were opposed to black emancipation. Some southerners and many northerners worked for the Bureau of Refugees, Freedmen, and Abandoned Lands, (the Freedmen's Bureau), created in 1865. Its agents helped blacks find jobs, obtain homes and land, and get an education. Lawyers working for the Bureau often defended the rights of freed blacks in court when they were arrested unfairly for breaking Black Codes.

You are one of the newly freed people in Texas who celebrate your freedom on Juneteenth. What will you do now that you are free? Where will you go? What job will you seek? What goals will you pursue? The decision is yours.

➤ To experience emancipation as a young black man fleeing to a new life, turn to page **13**.

➤ To be an African-American teenage girl looking for your family in neighboring Arkansas, turn to page **41**.

➤ To work as a young apprentice for a former slave master to help your family survive, turn to page **71**.

Freed blacks headed for Union territory after the Emancipation Proclamation in 1863. Texas slaves wouldn't learn of the freedom for two more years.

# CHAPTER 2

# On the Road to Freedom

It is June 19, 1865, in the city of Galveston, Texas. The long, bloody Civil War has been over for nearly two months. The South has lost to the North. But for you, a young black man on a plantation outside the city, little has changed. You are still a slave.

Today the slave cabins are buzzing with news. Yesterday federal troops arrived in Galveston to take over the city. What this will mean to you and thousands of other slaves in Texas, you don't yet know.

Your master, Mr. James, asks you and Sam— your friend and fellow slave—to go into town to buy supplies.

*Turn the page.*

You and Sam hitch up the horse to the wagon and head into Galveston. When you arrive you find the city in an uproar. There are throngs of people in the streets, along with federal soldiers in dark blue uniforms.

You quickly do your business at the store. When you come back out, you see a large crowd gathered around the Ashton Villa, a big brick house on 23rd Street and Broadway. You ask a white man standing nearby what's going on. "That blasted Yankee General Granger is about to speak," he says.

A loud murmur goes through the crowd as a soldier with a full beard steps out onto the balcony of the Ashton Villa.

"That must be old Granger," says Sam.

The crowd grows silent as General Granger begins to read from a paper in his hand. Your ears tingle when he reads the words:

"The people of Texas are informed that in accordance with a Proclamation from the Executive of the United States, all slaves are free."

Ashton Villa, site of General Granger's reading of the proclamation, was the first brick house to be built in Texas.

*Turn the page.*

You can't believe what you're hearing. Slaves around you, young and old, are dancing, singing, and laughing in the street. You and Sam join in.

"We're free!" Sam says, sinking to his knees in disbelief. "Free to go wherever we want!"

"Yes!" you cry. "Just as soon as we get these supplies back to Master's house."

"Forget him," says Sam. "We're not his slaves anymore."

What Sam says is true, but you feel you should take the supplies back. And anyway, you want to say good-bye to the other slaves.

"I think we should take the supplies back," you tell Sam.

"Let's leave them at the store with a message for Master," Sam says, "Then we can take off in the wagon. Think of the places we can go."

"But that would be stealing," you say to Sam.

"Come on, brother," says Sam. "Old James isn't going to miss that wagon much. Don't you want to see the world as a freedman?"

➤ To take the wagon with Sam, turn to page **18**.

➤ To strike off on your own without Sam, turn to page **21**.

You feel bad about taking Master James' wagon, but the attraction of freedom is stronger than your sense of right and wrong.

You and Sam make your way to the outskirts of Galveston. Within a few hours, you are stopped on a dusty road by a sheriff. "Where are you boys going with that wagon?" he asks.

➤ To tell him you're heading back to Master James' plantation, go to page **19**.

➤ To let Sam answer, turn to page **20**.

"Headed to Master James' plantation," you say.

"Hurry along then, boys," the sheriff says. Sam is disappointed as you head toward the plantation. But you are relieved not to be stealing.

By the time you get back, Master James is too busy dealing with the news of emancipation to ask where the supplies you were hauling have gone. He is not eager to lose his slaves, but he doesn't try to stop them from leaving. Sam goes to talk with the other slaves, but Master calls after you. "How would you like to stay on here to work for a while? For wages, of course," he says.

19

Having a job with pay may be a good way to start your new life. But, like Sam, you're eager to move on and see what freedom feels like.

➤ To accept Master James' offer, turn to page 22.

➤ To strike off on your own, turn to page 25.

Blacks farmed sweet potatoes and other crops at plantations throughout the South.

"Back to the plantation, just a few miles from here," Sam lies to the sheriff. When the sheriff insists on accompanying you there, Sam tries to change his story, but the sheriff doesn't buy it.

You finally admit you were stealing the wagon. You and Sam are put in jail and charged with theft. Your sentence is two years' hard labor. You foolishly threw away your newfound freedom and will have to wait two more years to get it back.

## THE END

*To follow another path, turn to page 11.*
*To read the conclusion, turn to page 101.*

You tell Sam he's welcome to do what he wants, but you won't risk being arrested for stealing. You plan to travel north, where you can blend in with other free blacks.

First you sneak back to your slave quarters to get your things. You don't want to see Mr. James or have to explain about Sam and the wagon.

You pack your personal items into a sack and swing your prized possession, your banjo, over your shoulder. You hope to use it to earn food or money on the journey.

*Turn to page 24.*

You agree to stay on, at least for a while. You are surprised to see that several other freed people have agreed to stay too. Among them is a girl your age named Luanne.

You have always liked Luanne but never had the nerve to tell her so. Becoming free has boosted your confidence. You court Luanne by taking her on picnics and long walks on Sunday afternoons. One night in early fall, you ask her to marry you. She accepts and you dream of building a free life together.

Now a married man, you work harder than ever. Master James is impressed by your work ethic and puts you in charge of other workers.

You and Luanne save your earnings. Within two years you have enough to start your own business, a small general store, in a nearby town. Master James is sorry to see the two of you leave, but he understands your desire to work for yourself.

Shortly after, Luanne gives birth to a boy. You're happy that your son will grow up a free man, never knowing the pains of slavery.

23

## THE END

*To follow another path, turn to page 11.*
*To read the conclusion, turn to page 101.*

You leave quietly, expecting that someone will try to stop you. You've never gone anywhere without permission. You walk and walk along the hot, dusty road.

Soon a white man in a ragged coat comes by on horseback. "Where are you headed, boy?" he asks you.

"Headed north," you tell him. "Sure wish I had a horse like yours to get me there."

Many freed blacks traveled on foot in search of jobs and new lives.

Turn to page **27**.

Mr. James is sorry to hear you want to leave, but he understands. You say good-bye to the other former slaves, who have been like family, and you walk away from your slave life.

You reach a small town a few miles to the north. There on the street you are surprised to bump into Sam.

"They're starting up a card game in the saloon," he tells you. "How about joining us?"

The only thing of worth you have is your banjo. Maybe you could bet with it and win enough to buy a train ticket north. But you could also end up losing your banjo.

➻ To play cards with Sam, turn to page **26**.
➻ To decline his offer and keep walking, turn to page **28**.

The idea of a train ticket convinces you to follow Sam into the saloon. It is filled with freed black men and women celebrating. You join three other men starting a poker game.

At first you do well and win several hands. But the temptation to keep winning leads to your downfall. Within an hour you have gambled away your banjo.

You leave the saloon. You won't be going north, not for a while. You had planned to earn your way there strumming banjo at saloons. Now you've got nothing. You shake your head at your first mistake as a free man.

## THE END

*To follow another path, turn to page 11.*
*To read the conclusion, turn to page 101.*

The man brings his horse to a halt. "I'll sell you my horse, Lucy, if you can meet my price," he says.

You have a few coins that you earned playing banjo. The man nods his head at your offer. You're surprised that he's willing to take so little, but you're thrilled at the idea of owning your own horse.

"She's a fine mare," he says. "Do we have a deal?"

To save your money and keep walking, turn to page **29**.

To buy the horse, turn to page **30**.

"Sorry," you say to Sam, "but I've got an appointment to keep."

"What appointment?" asks Sam.

"With the North. That's where I'm starting my new life as a free man and I've got no time for gambling."

You are pleased with yourself for resisting temptation. But what you are doing is a kind of gamble too. At least when you were a slave you knew you had plenty of food and a place to sleep—unlike at some other plantations you've heard about. Now you'll have to find those things on your own.

Days pass. Your feet are sore from walking. Once in a while, when you are lucky, you get a ride from a passing wagon for a few miles.

In Mississippi you pick up the Natchez Trace, an old Indian trail, and take it all the way to Nashville, Tennessee. Most nights you sleep outdoors and scrounge for food in the woods and fields. You find temporary work in a lumber mill and earn enough money to buy a ticket for a train to Baltimore, Maryland.

*Turn to page 35.*

You pay the man, and you have yourself a horse. "Enjoy your ride!" the man yells.

You do enjoy the ride, and before long you enter another small town. A white man sees you and calls out to some other men on the street. Soon the men are walking toward you, blocking the road. If you don't do what they say, you might get into trouble. White men are used to calling the shots. But will you be in deeper trouble if you stop?

➤ To stop and see what they want, go to page **31**.

➤ To keep riding out of town, turn to page **32**.

You bring Lucy to a stop. The men look at you with anger and suspicion. "Where did you get that horse, boy?" one of them asks.

"I bought her from a man down the road," you explain.

"He's lying!" cries another man. "That horse was stolen from my barn last night!"

You protest your innocence, but the mob isn't listening. They pull you off the horse, beat you, and then put you back on the horse. They tie your hands and put a noose around your neck. The other end of the rope is tied to a tree. You are about to be lynched. Your life as a free man ends before it even begins.

## THE END

*To follow another path, turn to page 11.*
*To read the conclusion, turn to page 101.*

You don't like the looks on the men's faces. You give the reins a shake and Lucy gallops out of town. After that, you try to avoid towns.

You eat wild roots and berries to survive. On a lucky day, you might catch a lazy fish for your dinner. You sleep outdoors, tying your horse to the nearest tree.

Days go by. As you approach the border of Arkansas and Tennessee, you see the mighty Mississippi River.

When able to save money for boat or train fare, many blacks headed north and west in the years following the Civil War.

There is a ferryboat that takes people across the river for a fee, but you don't have any money. You could sell Lucy to pay for the ferry. You might have enough money left to buy a train ticket once you reach the other side.

You would miss Lucy though. Besides, horses can swim. Maybe you could ford the river on her back. Time's wasting, and you've got to make a decision.

→ To sell your horse and ride the ferry, turn to page **34**.

→ To try to ford the river on horseback, turn to page **37**.

As much as you'd like to keep Lucy, your journey north is more important. You find a horse trader who buys the mare for a fair price. You board the ferry to Memphis and then buy a train ticket to Baltimore, Maryland.

On the train you head for the rear car, the only place where blacks are allowed to sit. You don't like being segregated, but it's not so important to you now that you know you're on your way to a new life in the city.

Baltimore is a bustling city but finding work is hard. Everyone, including many freedmen, seems to be looking for a job.

You decide to use your musical skills to get by until you can find work. You stand on a street corner, playing your banjo and singing songs. People like your music. Some even drop a little food or money into your hat.

One day a well-dressed black man stops to listen. "How would you like a job working in a minstrel show?" he asks after a song.

You've heard about minstrel shows and know they are racist. But how can you turn down an offer for a job?

→ To hold out for a different job, turn to page **36**.

→ To join the minstrel show, turn to page **38**.

You thank the man for the offer but tell him you don't think that's the life for you.

Over time you save up enough money to catch a train to New York City. It's the biggest city in the North, and you want to see it.

On a sunny morning in early September you arrive. You are happy to see people of many different cultures filling the streets.

You have only your banjo, the clothes on your back, and a few things in your sack, but you aren't worried. You know you will find work and a new life in this great city.

**36**

## THE END

*To follow another path, turn to page 11.*
*To read the conclusion, turn to page 101.*

You can't give up Lucy. You nudge her to the riverbank and kick her sides gently. She startles as she enters the chilly water.

The current is faster than you thought, and soon Lucy is struggling against it. You fall off the panicking horse and both of you are swimming for your lives.

You and Lucy both make it to shore, but she runs off, leaving you stranded. You are soaked to the skin. To make matters worse, you have lost everything—including your banjo—in the river. How will you support yourself without it? Your journey north has ended, for now.

## THE END

*To follow another path, turn to page 11.*
*To read the conclusion, turn to page 101.*

"I thought minstrel shows were all run by white people who blackened their faces," you say.

"That was true before the war," the man says. "But now there are several all-black minstrel shows run by blacks, such as myself."

He introduces himself as Amos Jones and gives you a free pass to watch his show that night. You watch black comics, dancers, singers, and musicians perform. In the final act, the troupe puts on a short play. But many of the acts make fun of blacks.

Blackface minstrel performer Charles H. King posed with a photo of himself without makeup visible on his shoe.

You wonder how the performers put up with it. Yet when the show plays the next night, you are in the orchestra, plucking away at your banjo.

You play in Baltimore for a week, and then the troupe travels to Philadelphia, New York, and Boston. You're not happy about the content of the minstrel shows, but you enjoy seeing these great cities. You also get paid enough money to buy new clothes and eat in black-owned restaurants.

You were once a poor slave from Texas, but now you are making a living as an entertainer. And someday, you hope, you'll leave the racist minstrel shows behind and play music on your own terms.

## THE END

*To follow another path, turn to page 11.*
*To read the conclusion, turn to page 101.*

Union troops occupied Texas in June 1865 and required slave owners to notify slaves of their freedom.

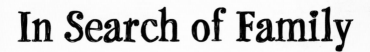

# CHAPTER 3

# In Search of Family

You are a teenage girl, a house slave, on a plantation north of Galveston, Texas. You work hard under the watchful eye of your mistress.

However, all that is about to change. It is June 20, 1865. This morning you are cleaning the master's bedroom when Eli, the old head servant, interrupts your work. "Come downstairs," he says. "Mistress has something to tell us."

Ann Fredericks, the master's wife, is standing in the drawing room, surrounded by the other house slaves. You don't think you've ever heard a kind word from her. But today she seems strangely nervous.

41

*Turn the page.*

Many generations lived together in small slave quarters on southern plantations.

"I have something to tell you," she says, her voice quavering. "The victors in the North have told us we have to free you. It is a terrible mistake, but as of now, if you choose, you are free to leave our home."

The words stun you. Free. You never thought it would happen, even after news arrived a month ago that the North had won the long war.

"Those of you who have good sense may stay and work for Master and me," continues Mrs. Fredericks. "We will pay you wages for your work, of course. I think that is the best choice for you."

You have no intention of staying. You want to find the family you lost when Master Fredericks sold your mother, brother, and sister to another slaveholder. It was years ago, but you still remember your mother's tearful face and her strong arms holding you for the last time. You still have the hat she left for you—the one thing she had to give.

There are only two people who know where they are. You follow one of them, Mrs. Fredericks, as she abruptly leaves the drawing room.

*Turn the page.*

"Yes?" says Mrs. Fredericks sharply. "What is it, girl?"

"Ma'am, I would like to find my family that Master sold off. Can you tell me where they be?"

"That was a long time ago," she replies. "I don't remember."

You dare to speak again. "Do you think Master would remember?"

"Master is very busy right now," she says. "Perhaps I can ask him later, if you decide to stay and work for us."

"Yes Ma'am," you say and leave the room. Hot tears flood your eyes. You don't want to stay, but what choice do you have now?

"Don't cry, child," says Eli, standing in the hallway. "I heard what Mistress said, but don't you worry. Eli knows where your kin are."

"You do?" you say, wiping your tears.

"Master sold them off to a man named Higgins who has a plantation over near Pine Bluff, Arkansas."

"How can I get there?" you ask.

"Well, a train would be fastest, but that costs money. You best go by foot. You should be able to find rides along the way."

You want to leave now and run to Arkansas, but if you stay a while, maybe you can earn money for a train ticket. Either way, you are determined to find your family.

➤ To earn money for a train ticket, turn to page **46**.

➤ To start now on foot, turn to page **48**.

You go to Mrs. Fredericks and tell her you would like to stay on and work for her. She seems relieved. Few of her other former slaves have taken up the offer.

Your life continues much as before. But now you are working as a freed woman. The Fredericks' wages are hardly generous, but you save every penny you earn.

Finally, you have enough money for the train ticket and a little extra for food. You tell Mrs. Fredericks you will be leaving. She isn't happy about it, but she cannot stop you.

Eli accompanies you to the train station in Galveston. You buy your ticket and hear the approaching train whistle. Eli gives you a warm hug. "Godspeed, child," he says.

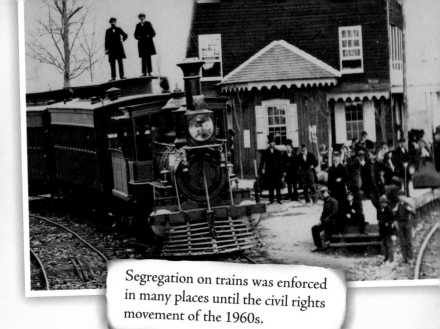

Segregation on trains was enforced in many places until the civil rights movement of the 1960s.

You get on the train. The conductor sees you and says, "All blacks to the rear car."

Although you are free, you are still subject to racism. As you walk through the car, a well-dressed white man with silver hair smiles and points to the empty seat next to him. Dare you take it?

❧ To sit next to the white gentleman, turn to page 50.

❧ To keep moving to the segregated car, turn to page 54.

You decide to start your journey to Arkansas on foot. Eli sets you on the right road. "Just keep following the road north and when you get to Arkansas, you can ask from there," he tells you.

You are surprised to see many other freed blacks on the road. Some are on foot. Others are riding horses or walking alongside horse-pulled carts. They are all headed to Houston, the nearest large city. They sing and laugh and share food as they walk along. You are relieved to have company.

The afternoon fades and you grow tired and thirsty. You come to the outskirts of a town and see trees and grass. Many of the group you're traveling with take a break and rest under the shady trees.

Maybe you should stay with the group and rest awhile too. But you're eager to keep going and get to the next town before nightfall.



*To keep going, turn to page* **52**.

*To stay with the group, turn to page* **57**.

You nervously sit down next to the white man. "Where are you headed, young lady?" he asks kindly, calming your nerves.

You explain how you are going to find your family in Arkansas. As you finish your story, the conductor comes by and glares at you. "Didn't I tell you that all blacks sit in the rear cars?" The man next to you holds up a card. The conductor apologizes and quickly moves away.

"Who are you, sir?" you ask him.

"I'm a detective for the railroad," he explains. He sees the surprised look on your face. "Oh, don't worry," he says. "I'm not going to arrest you. On the contrary, I want to help."

"I watch out for freed blacks on the train," he explains. "When the train gets to Little Rock, I'll do some investigating and see where the Higgins' place is. Maybe I can even take you there."

The man reminds you a little of Eli. You want to believe that he's telling you the truth. You want to believe that not all white people are bad.

The train ride is long, and you want to take a nap. Maybe you should move to the back of the train with the blacks. Will you be safer there while you sleep?

⇒ *To go to sleep, turn to page* **56**.

⇒ *To move to the back of the train, turn to page* **62**.

You decide to keep going on your own. You walk for hours, growing tired and hungry. The sun begins to set in the west, and you're getting nervous about spending a night alone on the roadside. You continue on, looking for a safe spot, regretting your decision to travel by yourself.

As if in answer to your prayers, a horse-drawn wagon comes rumbling down the road. A black boy about your age is sitting in the driver's seat. In the back of the wagon are a dozen black people.

Travel by horse and wagon was slow. About 15 to 20 miles per day was an average pace.

"Where you headed, girl?" the boy asks.

"To Arkansas," you reply.

"That's a long way. We're going to Beaumont. I can take you that far if you like."

That sounds good to you. You head for the back of the wagon, but the boy says, "It's crowded back there. Why don't you sit up here with me?" You're not sure if that's a good idea.



*To sit in the back, turn to page* **60**.

*To sit up front with the driver, turn to page* **63**.

You make your way through the cars to the last one, reserved for black passengers. You take a seat next to a large woman holding a small boy. Something about him reminds you of your brother. The last time you saw him he was about that age. Would you even recognize him now?

The train chugs along the tracks, and you close your eyes to rest. You hear the woman humming an old spiritual to her son. It's a song your mother used to sing to you. You never dared hope you would see her again, and now you have a chance.

You arrive in Little Rock, Arkansas, and get off the train. It's a bustling capital city of nearly 4,000 people.

You ask a man working at the station how you can get to Pine Bluff.

The man scratches his beard. "Well now, you want fancy or you want cheap? There's a stagecoach that goes there, for a price. Or you can travel down the Arkansas River by flatboat. Costs less, but it will be crowded."

➤ *To take the stagecoach, turn to page **64**.*

➤ *To take the flatboat, turn to page **65**.*

You notice that the man is also dozing. You tuck your purse under your arm and soon are fast asleep.

When a whistle from the train wakes you, it is growing dark outside. The detective is gone, and so is your purse! In a panic you ask the conductor if he's seen him.

"Sure did," he says. "Turns out he's no railroad detective. He's a pickpocket and I threw him off. And now you better move back where you belong, or I'll throw you off too!"

You feel sick. All your money was in that purse. As you wonder what you'll do next, you miss your mother more than ever.

## THE END

*To follow another path, turn to page 11.*
*To read the conclusion, turn to page 101.*

You find a place to stretch out under a large elm tree and are soon fast asleep. You are dreaming of your mother when suddenly a kick on the foot awakens you. "Get up, girl," says a low, male voice.

You open your eyes and see a tall white man with a badge pinned to his vest standing over you.

"You're under arrest for vagrancy."

You try to explain that you were only resting for a short time before moving on. But the sheriff isn't listening.

*Turn the page.*

He marches you and others from your group to the jail, already crowded with blacks also charged with vagrancy. "This law is just a way for them to keep us in our place," one woman says.

The next day you appear in court and must pay a fine or spend a month in jail. You pay the fine, but now you are penniless and far from Arkansas and your family. Maybe the new life you envisioned is nothing but a dream.

## THE END

*To follow another path, turn to page 11.*
*To read the conclusion, turn to page 101.*

Freed blacks often traveled in groups for safety and company after leaving plantations.

You get into the back with the others. As you squeeze between two people, you hear someone say your name. You are shocked to look up and see your sister, Sally! You hug and cry tears of joy. You spend the rest of the ride telling one another about your lives since you were separated years ago. Now you are both looking for your mother.

In Beaumont you find other travelers on the road to Arkansas willing to take you and Sally as passengers. It takes several more weeks, but you finally arrive in Pine Bluff. You get directions to the Higgins' plantation and head directly for it.

Nervously you and Sally walk up the long driveway to the main house. A black servant answers the door.

"Does Annie still work here?" you ask.

The servant stares at you. "There's no Annie here. Never has been." He pauses, then says, "You must be thinking of Mr. Higgins' brother, John. The Union soldiers burned him out."

Your heart drops in your chest. "But what about the slaves, I mean ex-slaves?"

"Sorry. House and property were all destroyed. If the slaves survived, they ran off."

You cling to Sally. The search for your mother has come to a tragic end.

## THE END

*To follow another path, turn to page 11.*
*To read the conclusion, turn to page 101.*

You thank the man for his offer to help and tell him you'll look for him at the station. You find a seat in the back and fall asleep.

When the train stops in Pine Bluff, you ask the conductor where the detective has gone.

"Detective! Turned out to be a con man," he tells you. "He stole someone's wallet and got off at the last station."

You can't believe you almost trusted that liar. Determined to never trust a white man again, you approach the first black man you see in Pine Bluff.

*Turn to page 68.*

You climb up alongside the driver, Henry, who chats away while the other passengers doze in the back. "You sure are pretty," he says after a while. His words embarrass you and you say nothing.

"How about a little kiss for ol' Henry, huh?" he says. He leans over, but you push him away.

"What's the matter?" he hisses. "I just wanted a kiss!" In a rage, he pushes you off the wagon. In the dark, the sleepy passengers never even see you fall. The wagon rumbles off.

You've hurt your ankle and will walk the rest of your life with a limp. But when you are finally reunited with your mother months later, you know that all your struggles were worth it.

## THE END

*To follow another path, turn to page 11.*
*To read the conclusion, turn to page 101.*

The stagecoach is faster, and you're eager to get to Pine Bluff. You buy your ticket. Because you are black, you aren't allowed to sit inside with the white passengers. Instead, you sit outside, beside the driver. It's a rough ride, and you feel every bump in the road.

You arrive at Pine Bluff late in the day. You see a middle-aged black man loading a wagon. You approach him, hoping that he's familiar with the town.

Turn to page 68.

The flatboat is crowded with goods, animals, crew members, and other passengers. Most of them are poor freed blacks like you.

You're crowded near the edge, and a sudden gust of wind blows your hat off your head and into the water. Your mother's hat! If you jump in after it, you can still retrieve it. The water doesn't look too deep and surely the crew will help you back aboard. But you know that jumping in will cause a ruckus.

➤ *To jump into the water, turn to page 66.*

➤ *To let the hat go, turn to page 67.*

You leap over the side of the boat and hit the chilly water. You quickly swim to your hat. But as you grab it, you feel an undertow pulling you downward. The people on the boat are yelling to you, but you can't hear their words.

Someone throws you a rope, but it is too short and you can't reach it. The current pulls you down, down to the muddy depths of the river. In trying to save your mother's hat, you've lost the chance to be with her again.

## THE END

*To follow another path, turn to page 11.*
*To read the conclusion, turn to page 101.*

Families were often cruelly separated at slave auctions. After emancipation many former slaves searched for lost family members.

It's only a hat, you tell yourself. It's your mother that you really want.

The flatboat continues down the Arkansas River. You spend a rather uncomfortable night sleeping on deck. The next morning you arrive in Pine Bluff. As you leave the flatboat, you see a black man loading goods from the boat onto a wagon.

*Turn the page.*

"Do you know the Higgins' plantation?" you ask him.

He smiles. "I guess I ought to, since I work there." Your heart leaps. You ask if he knows Annie.

"I sure do, but she left the place a couple of months ago with the emancipation."

You feel a sharp pain in your chest. Have you come all this way to lose your mother again? "Do you know where she went?" you ask.

"Why, she's right here in Pine Bluff, working for the American Missionary Society," he says. "They opened up a school for black children. Annie's one of the teachers there. What's she to you?"

"She's my mama!" you exclaim.

The kind man takes you directly to the school. You thank him and enter the small building, your heart beating fast.

A tall black woman is standing and reading from a book to several black children. She looks up and asks, "May I help you?"

"Mama," you say, stepping closer. "Don't you recognize me?"

She stares at you for a long moment then says, "Mercy!" and drops her book to the floor. She runs to hug you. "I knew you'd come!" she cries. "I stayed here in Pine Bluff, knowing you'd come find me! I prayed Eli would tell you where to look!"

You keep hugging and won't let go. Whatever challenges lie ahead, you will face them together.

**69**

## THE END

*To follow another path, turn to page 11.*
*To read the conclusion, turn to page 101.*

Freedmen's Schools, set up by the Freedmen's Bureau, were established for blacks, whose education was essential to succeed as free people.

# CHAPTER 4

# A Slave Once More?

It has been two months since you and your family, along with thousands of other slaves in Texas, were freed. But freedom has not been as wonderful as you thought it would be. Your parents both work hard at odd jobs to support your family. You go to the new school for ex-slave children started by a government group called the Freedmen's Bureau. But life at home is hard with little to eat.

One day your parents ask to speak with you. They look serious. You hope they aren't about to punish you for putting that frog in your sister's bed.

*Turn the page.*

"Son," your father says, "we're facing a tough time right now. If we don't find a way to earn more, we'll lose our home."

You knew things were bad, but you didn't think they were that bad.

"We all have to pull our weight," Pa continues. "You're old enough to get a job. We know how much you enjoy school, but this would only be for a year, until we're back on our feet."

You do like school, but you would do anything to help your family. "What would I do?" you ask.

"A lot of the planters around here are having a hard time running their plantations without slaves working their fields," Pa says. "They're hiring young people to live and work there as apprentices. Your wages would help us get by."

"Would I be able to come home every night?" you ask.

"No, son," says your mother, about to cry. "It'd be too far away to come home every night. But maybe on Sundays …"

"Yes, we'll see about that," says Pa patting Mother's arm. "There are two men I've contacted about hiring you on. One is our old master, Mr. Malloy. The other is a man named Anderson."

*Turn the page.*

"I don't want him working for Malloy," says Mother. "He's used to us being his slaves, and I don't think he'd treat our son as a free person."

"But Mr. Malloy was a good master," your father points out. "And he knows the boy and likes him."

"I'd rather see him work for this Anderson," Mother says. "He has a smaller plantation and only had a few slaves."

Pa sighs and turns to you. "Well, I think you should be the one to decide. Who do you want to work for?"

You're not sure. You liked Mr. Malloy well enough, but working on a smaller plantation might be easier.

➤ To work for Mr. Malloy, go to page 75.

➤ To work for Mr. Anderson, turn to page 77.

That Sunday you and your parents set off on the long walk to the Malloys. Mother holds your hand tightly the whole way.

Mr. Malloy is happy to see you and signs a work contract with your father. You will work for him for one year. Every month your father will get your wages. Mr. Malloy will provide you with room and board.

When it's time for your parents to leave, Mother hugs you tightly. "Be a good boy," she says tearfully, "and we'll see you soon." You're not sure when that will be.

*Turn the page.*

Mr. Malloy takes you to the big barn where workers are cleaning cotton. A burly white man with a beard greets him.

"Boy, this is Mr. Tucker," Mr. Malloy says. "He's my new overseer. You'll be answering to him."

"Nice to meet you," says Tucker, but as soon as Mr. Malloy leaves, the smile vanishes from Tucker's face. "Let's get one thing straight, boy," he says. "I'm the boss here and you do what I say or there'll be trouble. Understand?"

You understand all right, and you don't like this man at all. He's acting like you're still a slave. How do you respond to his question?

→ To give in to Tucker, turn to page 79.

→ To stand up for yourself, turn to page 82.

Freed blacks worked for meager pay at jobs slaves used to perform.

The Anderson farm is far smaller than the Malloy plantation, and the house isn't half as big as the Malloy mansion. Mrs. Anderson, a large, hefty woman, is feeding the chickens in the yard when you arrive. Mr. Anderson comes out of the farmhouse.

He welcomes you warmly and tells your parents that you are going to get along fine. Your mother seems relieved. She talks to Mrs. Anderson as your father and Mr. Anderson go over your work contract.

*Turn the page.*

You are sad to see your parents leave, but you try not to think about it.

You eat with the two other apprentices. A black house worker cooks you fried chicken with dumplings and sweet potatoes. Then you head to your bed of straw in the barn.

Tired after a long day, you quickly fall asleep. You dream about home and how life will be better in the future when your family has enough to live on.

Suddenly you are awakened by a kick in the back. You sit up with a start. Mr. Anderson is standing over you, looking anything but friendly.

78

*Turn to page* **80**.

"I understand," you say, lowering your head.

"Good," says Tucker. "And don't forget it."

He takes you out to the cotton fields and puts you to work. Picking cotton is hard labor, but it's Tucker's threatening presence in the fields that makes it unbearable. You listen as he yells at one apprentice and strikes another with his whip for working too slowly. You can see this year as an apprentice will be a difficult one—one that feels a lot like slavery. The only thing that keeps you going is knowing you are helping your family to a better life.

79

## THE END

*To follow another path, turn to page 11.*
*To read the conclusion, turn to page 101.*

"Get up! I called you three times. It's time for work!" he barks.

The change in Mr. Anderson shocks you. He seemed so nice yesterday, and now he couldn't be meaner. Was his being nice all an act for your parents? You hurry out to the field, where you are handed a hoe.

"Start breaking up this ground," commands Mr. Anderson. He is a different person from the man you met yesterday. You strike at the hard earth with the hoe. Hours pass. Every time you start to slow down, Mr. Anderson comes around and tells you to work faster. It's still another hour to lunchtime. You are bone tired, thirsty, and need a break.

Freed blacks sometimes stayed on their plantations to work because they had nowhere else to go.

Mr. Anderson has gone back to the house. You really need to sit down, just for a few minutes. But do you dare?

→ To take a rest, turn to page **84**.

→ To keep working until lunch, turn to page **86**.

To Tucker's amazement, you shake your head. "I'm not your slave, Mr. Tucker," you say. "I'm a free person and you can't talk to me that way."

Tucker laughs to hide his surprise at your boldness. "You hear that, boys?" he says to the other black workers. "He's a free man!"

The men mumble and turn away. They may be under Tucker's control, but they don't like him any more than you do.

"I'll show you how free you are," mutters the overseer.

Tucker pulls back his whip and lashes out at you. The whiplash stings the skin of your chest right through your shirt. You cry out, but the other apprentices just turn away.

The overseer flicks back the whip again. It is thick and heavy. If you try, you might be able to grab it from him when it strikes you. But maybe it would be better to just turn and run. Surely Mr. Malloy will come to your defense.

→ To try to grab the whip, turn to page **87**.

→ To turn and run, turn to page **90**.

You sit down and rest your head on your knees. It feels so good to be off your feet. You close your eyes and tell yourself you'll get up in a few minutes.

It feels like your eyes have just closed when you hear a man's shout. You open your eyes to see Mr. Anderson standing over you. "Sleeping on the job, huh?" he says. "I'll teach you not to do that again!"

He picks up a small sack of grain and swings it at you as the two other apprentices watch. The sack hits you hard on the side, and you gasp in pain. He strikes you half a dozen more times. You want to cry out with each blow, but you don't.

"Now get back to work or there'll be more of the same, boy!"

You work until lunchtime and then all through the afternoon, despite the pain in your ribs. When the workday is over, you are exhausted. You can hardly lift your hand to eat your dinner. As you crawl onto your straw bed, you know you can't take another day like this. You decide you will run back home to your parents.

At midnight you gather your things in a small bag and quietly slip out of the barn. You can take the road or you can make your way home through the woods. The road is faster but risky, because other people might see you. However, there probably won't be too many travelers on it at night.

➧ *To take the woods, turn to page **88**.*

➧ *To take the road, turn to page **92**.*

You keep scratching away at the ground with the hoe. When lunchtime comes, you are feeling faint and can't eat a thing. But Mr. Anderson sends you back to work. He says you are making excuses.

You go back to the field, dizzy from your aching head. Within an hour you pass out. The apprentice driving the team of oxen doesn't see you lying in the dirt until it's too late.

## THE END

*To follow another path, turn to page 11.*
*To read the conclusion, turn to page 101.*

As the whip comes at you, you lunge at Tucker and seize the handle with both hands. Tucker tries to pull it back, but you hold tight and yank it from his grasp. Just then Mr. Malloy enters the barn. "What in blazes is going on here?"

Tucker accuses you of attacking him. You insist that you were only defending yourself. The other workers are too afraid to say a word.

"I'm sorry, boy," Mr. Malloy says, "but I'm going to have to dismiss you."

You have lost your job and may not get another one. You have let your family down. You wonder if life as a freedman will always be this hard.

87

## THE END

*To follow another path, turn to page 11.*
*To read the conclusion, turn to page 101.*

You enter the woods. You hear the low growl of some wild animal, but you keep walking. By daybreak, you reach home. It never looked so good. Your parents are stunned to see you.

"What happened, son?" Pa asks. You tell them about the beating and beg not to go back.

"You won't have to," your father replies.

Your mother makes you something to eat from what little she has, and then you fall gratefully into your bed.

Freed blacks had little to no money and made homes in small cabins or shacks.

The next day two men appear in your yard, one in a wagon and one on horseback. It's Mr. Anderson and the sheriff. You stay with your mother in the cabin while your father goes out to meet them.

"Your boy ran away and I've come to fetch him," you hear Anderson say.

"He ran away because you beat him," Pa replies.

"He's a liar," says Anderson.

"Mr. Anderson has a signed contract," says the sheriff. "You have to turn him over."

"He's not here," Pa says. Anderson asks the sheriff to search the cabin.

Mother tells you to hide in the woods behind the house. But that might get your parents into deeper trouble.

➤ To hide in the woods, turn to page **91**.

➤ To go outside and turn yourself in, turn to page **93**.

You run for the barn door and Tucker follows, whip in hand. You run right into Mr. Malloy. Tucker stops dead in his tracks.

"What's going on?" asks Mr. Malloy.

"The boy tried to attack me," Tucker says.

"Is this true, boy?" Mr. Malloy asks you.

"No, sir. He yelled at me for no cause and I told him he couldn't. Then he beat me with the whip."

You can tell that Malloy believes you. "I'm sure it was just a misunderstanding, right Tucker?" Malloy says. Tucker nods.

**90**

You know working for Tucker will be hard, but you are proud that you stood up for yourself. You're not a slave anymore.

## THE END

*To follow another path, turn to page 11.*
*To read the conclusion, turn to page 101.*

You run out the back door and hide behind a tree. You peek around and see the sheriff put handcuffs on Pa and then drive him away in Anderson's wagon. Mr. Anderson follows, leading the sheriff's horse. Mother is crying.

You feel terrible as you realize that your father is going to be punished because you ran away. You wish you had stayed at Anderson's farm. Nothing that could happen to you there could be as awful as this.

## THE END

*To follow another path, turn to page 11.*
*To read the conclusion, turn to page 101.*

Ku Klux Klan members didn't support emancipation. They attacked blacks and sometimes wore white hoods to hide their identities.

You decide you won't get lost so easily if you stick to the road. You've gone about a mile when you hear men's voices up ahead in the dark. They are laughing and talking. Four white men come into view and spot you in the moonlight. They stop and stare at you. What do you do?

➤ To turn and run away, turn to page **94**.

➤ To try to bluff your way past them, turn to page **98**.

You can't run and hide. You don't want your parents to be blamed for something you did. You open the door and step outside.

"So, he's not here?" Mr. Anderson says to Pa. "Come on, boy. It's a long walk for you back to my farm. You better get started."

Just then a third man rides up on horseback. "Hold on," the man says. "That boy's not going anywhere."

"Who says so?" asks Mr. Anderson with a scowl.

"The Freedmen's Bureau," the man replies.

➺ *Turn to page* **95**.

You turn and run as fast as your legs will carry you. You hear the men calling out. You are sure you can outrun them, but you trip on a rock and tumble to the ground. As you scramble back up, one of them tackles you.

"Where you running to, boy?" he asks.

You try to lie, but you panic and they figure out you're a runaway. They take you to the sheriff, who holds you in the jail overnight. Word goes out about a runaway apprentice, and Mr. Anderson comes to the jail the next day to claim you. You know you're in for another beating when you get back to his place.

## THE END

*To follow another path, turn to page 11.*
*To read the conclusion, turn to page 101.*

You've heard your father talk about the Freedmen's Bureau. It protects the rights of former slaves and tries to help them get started on their own.

"This isn't any of your business, Mr. Phelps," says the sheriff, who seems to know the stranger. "Mr. Anderson has a legal contract with this family."

"But contracts can be broken by both sides," says Mr. Phelps. "Mr. Johnson here contacted me yesterday to speak on his son's behalf. The Bureau feels this case should be decided by the courts."

"You'll get a chance to make your case in court," the sheriff tells Anderson as they ride away.

*Turn the page.*

You find out that Mr. Phelps is a lawyer. "Do you have marks on your body you can show me from the beating Anderson gave you?" he asks.

You take off your shirt, but there are only a few minor bruises.

"Anderson is a clever man," says Mr. Phelps. "He knows better than to use a whip. A whip leaves cuts and scars. A sack of grain doesn't."

"How are we going to prove it?" your Pa asks. You think of the other apprentices. Would they be willing to testify against Anderson? You doubt they would take your side against their employer, but they might if Mr. Phelps talks to them.

➤ To not bother mentioning the other apprentices, go to page **97**.

➤ To tell Mr. Phelps about the apprentices, turn to page **99**.

A few days later, your case is heard by the judge. Anderson's lawyer talks about the legal contract that your father signed. The judge listens and nods his head. Mr. Phelps tries to make a case against Mr. Anderson, but he has no hard evidence to prove his cruelty.

The judge decides in favor of Anderson. You hear Mother crying as you are taken out of the courtroom by the sheriff and put on Mr. Anderson's wagon. The law has let you down, and you will serve your time under your cruel employer. It will be a long year, if you survive.

## THE END

*To follow another path, turn to page 11.*
*To read the conclusion, turn to page 101.*

You decide that running from these men will only arouse their suspicions. You will keep your cool.

"Where you going at this hour, boy?" one asks.

"To my master's house," you say slowly. "If I don't get there soon he'll give me some beating!"

The men laugh. "You'd better hurry home or we'll beat you for him!" another one says.

"Yes, sir!" you reply and move on down the road past them. You give a deep sigh of relief. You fooled those men and escaped capture. You continue to walk all night.

**98**

Finally you arrive home and your surprised parents greet you with open arms. You tell them what happened. Your father vows he won't let anyone treat you as a slave.

## THE END

*To follow another path, turn to page 11.*
*To read the conclusion, turn to page 101.*

You tell Mr. Phelps about the other apprentices. He goes to the farm and convinces two of them to speak against Anderson.

The day of the trial, Mr. Phelps calls the two apprentices to the stand. They tell how they saw Anderson beat you. They also say how he has beaten them many times.

The judge says the contract is invalid because of Mr. Anderson's abuse. He releases you from his employment. You rush to Mother's arms as Pa gives Mr. Phelps a hug.

Mr. Phelps tells you the Freedmen's Bureau will find you an employer who will treat you better. You nod, ready to go to work to help your family.

**99**

## THE END

*To follow another path, turn to page 11.*
*To read the conclusion, turn to page 101.*

Freed blacks gathered in Washington, D.C., in 1866 to celebrate the abolition of slavery. Juneteenth celebrations began that year in Texas and spread throughout the South in later years.

# CHAPTER 5

# A National Celebration

Juneteenth Day became a day of remembrance and celebration of African-American freedom in Texas in 1866—the year after the first Juneteenth. Former slaves and their descendants made a yearly pilgrimage to Galveston to celebrate Juneteenth. The tradition of celebration spread to other southern states and grew more and more elaborate over time. Events included parades, rodeos, street fairs, family reunions, picnics, barbecues, prayer services, historical reenactments, and even beauty contests.

Musicians performed at a Juneteenth celebration in Austin, Texas, in 1900.

But in some towns and cities, white authorities wouldn't allow African-Americans to celebrate on public lands. So they moved the festivals to more rural areas and black church grounds. In time, freed blacks were able to buy land and donate it for Juneteenth celebrations. One black minister raised $1,000 from his congregation to buy public land in Houston, Texas, that became Emancipation Park.

Other parks sprang up in the cities of Austin and Mexia. Thousands of African-Americans came to these parks for Juneteenth celebrations that lasted as long as a week.

By the beginning of the 1900s, Juneteenth celebrations had largely disappeared. The early history of emancipation was fading for many younger African-Americans, who wanted to forget about the days of slavery.

When the Great Depression struck in the 1930s, many southern blacks moved from the country to cities to look for work in factories. Some blacks may well have felt there was little left to celebrate.

Equal rights for African-Americans were stifled years before by Jim Crow laws in the South. These laws prevented black people from using public facilities meant for whites and kept their schools and other institutions segregated. They supported the legal racism started by the earlier Black Codes. Segregation was a part of everyday life in many parts of the country.

Finally, in the 1950s, the fight for civil rights was ignited by a bus strike in Birmingham, Alabama, which made civil rights activist Dr. Martin Luther King Jr. a national figure. Nonviolent sit-ins and marches by both blacks and whites were often met with violence by white racists and police in the South. But times were changing, and civil rights were being won. The Civil Rights Act of 1964 and the Voting Rights Act of 1965 finally gave black Americans the rights they had been promised 100 years earlier.

With the push for black equality came the return of Juneteeth. The Reverend Ralph Abernathy, leader of the Poor People's Campaign in Washington, D.C., in 1968, called for a revival of Juneteenth celebrations.

On January 1, 1980, a law was passed in Texas to establish Juneteenth as a state holiday. The effort was led by African-American state lawmaker Al Edwards. He saw it as his mission to spearhead laws in other states to make Juneteenth a holiday.

More than 40 states and the District of Columbia now recognize June 19 as Juneteenth and celebrate it as either a state holiday or a special day of observance. The Smithsonian Institution in Washington, D.C., and other museums and cultural institutions sponsor Juneteenth activities on this special day.

The year 2015 marks the 150th anniversary of Juneteenth. The day that emancipation came to Texas 150 years ago has become a day of remembrance and dedication. It's a day not just for African-Americans, but for all Americans who believe in justice and equality.

# Timeline

**January 1, 1863**—The Emancipation Proclamation is announced by President Abraham Lincoln, releasing all slaves from bondage in the Confederacy. However, with the Civil War still being fought, no slaves are freed.

**April 9, 1865**—Confederate general Robert E. Lee surrenders to Union general Ulysses S. Grant at Appomattox Court House, Virginia, effectively ending the Civil War.

**June 18, 1865**—General Gordon Granger arrives in Galveston, Texas, with 2,000 federal troops to enforce the emancipation of slaves in the state.

**June 19, 1865**—Granger reads "General Order No. 3" in public, ending slavery in Texas. This day has come to be called Juneteenth.

**June 19, 1866**—The first official Juneteenth celebrations take place in Galveston and other Texas towns and cities.

**June 1968**—During the Poor People's Campaign in Washington, D.C., civil rights leader Ralph Abernathy encourages African-Americans to rededicate themselves to celebrating Juneteenth.

**January 1, 1980**—Juneteenth becomes an official state holiday in Texas.

**1997**—U.S. Congress passes legislation that recognizes Juneteenth Independence Day in the United States.

**January 20, 2009**—Barack Obama, the first black president of the United States, is inaugurated.

**June 19, 2015**—The nation commemorates the 150th anniversary of emancipation in Texas, Juneteenth.

# OTHER PATHS TO EXPLORE

In this book you've seen how the events surrounding emancipation of the slaves in Texas look different from several points of view.

Perspectives on history are as varied as the people who lived it. You can explore other paths on your own to learn more about what happened. Seeing history from many points of view is an important part of understanding it.

- Without slave labor, some plantations could no longer operate. Why do you think many white southerners resented freed slaves? (Key Ideas and Details)

- The Freedmen's Bureau helped freed slaves and protected them from white abuse. What do you think motivated these people to help African-Americans? What good came from their efforts in the South? (Craft and Structure)

- With the war over, many people headed west to find new opportunities and land. The Native Americans who lived there were pushed farther west. What do you think the native peoples thought of emancipation and the people who came to their land? (Integration of Knowledge and Ideas)

# READ MORE

**Hall, Brianna.** *Freedom From Slavery: Causes and Effects of the Emancipation Proclamation.* North Mankato, Minn.: Capstone Press, 2014.

**Hermann, Spring.** *The Struggle for Freedom.* Chicago: Heinemann-Raintree, 2010.

**Johnson, Angela.** *All Different Now: Juneteenth, the First Day of Freedom.* New York: Simon & Schuster Books for Young Readers, 2014.

**Peppas, Lynn.** *Juneteenth.* New York: Crabtree Publishing, 2011.

# INTERNET SITES

Use FactHound to find Internet sites related to this book. All of the sites on FactHound have been researched by our staff.

Here's all you do:
Visit *www.facthound.com*
Type in this code: 9781491418024

# GLOSSARY

**abolish** (uh-BOL-ish)—to put an end to

**apprentice** (uh-PREN-tiss)—someone who learns a trade or craft by working with a skilled person

**emancipation** (i-MAN-si-pay-shuhn)—the freeing from bondage of a people, such as African-American slaves

**ford** (FORD)—to cross a body of water

**minstrel show** (MIN-struhl SHOW)—a variety show popular in the 19th and early 20th centuries in the United States in which white performers often wore black makeup on their faces

**overseer** (OH-vur-see-uhr)—a supervisor of workers

**plantation** (plan-TAY-shuhn)—a large farm where usually a single crop is grown, such as tobacco or cotton

**racism** (RAY-si-zim)—the belief that one race is better than others

**segregation** (seg-ruh-GAY-shuhn)—the practice of keeping groups of people apart, especially based on race

**spiritual** (SPEER-ih-chu-uhl)—a type of religious song first sung by African-American slaves in the South

**vagrancy** (VAY-gruhn-see)—wandering from place to place without money or work

# BIBLIOGRAPHY

**Berlin, Ira, and Leslie S. Rowland.** *Families and Freedom.* New York: The New Press, 1997.

**Chunchang, Gao.** *African-Americans in the Reconstruction Era.* New York: Garland Publishing, 2000.

**Crouch, Barry A.** *The Dance of Freedom: Texas African-Americans During Reconstruction.* Austin: University of Texas Press, 2007.

**Juneteenth.** The Handbook of Texas Online. Texas State Historical Association. 4 Nov. 2014. www.tshaonline.org/handbook/online/articles/lkj01

**Juneteenth World Wide Celebration.** 4 Nov. 2014. www.juneteenth.com/

**The Minstrel Show.** Roy Rosenzweig Center for History and New Media. 4 Nov. 2014. http://chnm.gmu.edu/ courses/jackson/minstrel/minstrel.html

**Regosin, Elizabeth.** *Freedom's Promise: Ex-Slave Families and Citizenship in the Age of Emancipation.* Charlottesville: University Press of Virginia, 2002.

# INDEX